To Lead, First Be Human

By

Otsuko Notoma

Copyright © Otsuko Notoma 2025

All Rights Reserved

No part of this publication may be reproduced, distributed, or transmitted in any form or by any means, including photocopying, recording, or other electronic or mechanical methods, without the author's prior written permission, except in the case of brief quotations embodied in critical reviews and certain other non-commercial uses permitted by copyright law. For permission requests, please get in touch with the author.

Table of Contents

DEDICATION I

ACKNOWLEDGEMENT II

ABOUT THE AUTHOR: III

FOREWORD IV

INTRODUCTION THE QUIET RECKONING 1

CHAPTER 1 THE WEIGHT OF A TITLE 5

CHAPTER 2 THE POWER OF SMALL ACTS 10

CHAPTER 3 LEADERS ARE MADE, NOT BORN 15

CHAPTER 4 LEADING THROUGH RESISTANCE 19

CHAPTER 5 PEOPLE ARE THE MISSION 24

CHAPTER 6 THE LIE OF THE ALL-KNOWING LEADER 30

CHAPTER 7 EMOTIONAL LABOR IS REAL WORK 36

CHAPTER 8 THE COST OF THE ROLE 43

CHAPTER 9 THE GREATEST LIE WE TELL OURSELVES 49

CHAPTER 10 LEADERSHIP IS A HUMAN UNDERTAKING 56

CONCLUSION TO LEAD, FIRST BE HUMAN 64

COMING SOON: KEEP WALKING HOW SMALL STEPS BUILD A BIG LIFE ...67

Dedication

To my dearest wife and children,

This book is as much yours as it is mine. Your love, patience, and unwavering support have been the foundation that allowed me to walk this path. My darling wife has been my anchor, my steady reminder that courage and care must always walk together. Both my children taught me that laughter and curiosity are daily proof of why the human heart matters more than any title or achievement.

Everything I write here, I dedicate to you, with gratitude that cannot be measured and love that knows no end.

Acknowledgement

I would like to honor the people who have shaped my journey and whose presence has been an enduring light.

To my mother, whose late pursuit of her nursing certification taught me that growth never has an expiration date. And to my father, whose relentless dedication to learning instilled in me a belief that knowledge is not just for advancement but for transformation. Their lives are a testament that perseverance and faith carry us further than circumstance ever could.

And to every colleague, friend, and leader who walked beside me, whether in encouragement, in challenge, or in quiet example, thank you. Your influence is stitched into these pages. The lessons I share are not mine alone; they are echoes of the people who showed me what it means to lead with humanity first.

About the Author:

Ogheneotsuko K. Notoma holds a Doctor of Technology from Purdue University, earned while balancing full-time leadership responsibilities, fatherhood, and global service. His academic journey also includes multiple graduate degrees in information security and assurance, as well as a host of industry-recognized certifications in cybersecurity and technology governance. A committed lifelong learner, Notoma's educational path reflects both the rigor of discipline and the resilience of purpose. It is proof that it is never too late to reach the pinnacle of academic and professional growth.

Foreword

I didn't write this book because I see myself as a great leader. In fact, I wrote it precisely because I don't. I've spent decades working under, alongside, and sometimes in spite of leaders. I've watched leadership succeed, falter, inspire, and disappoint. Through it all, I've come to understand that real leadership isn't about having all the answers, holding the highest rank, or commanding the loudest voice in the room. It's about presence. It's about people. It's about the courage to care, even when no one's looking.

Throughout my career, I've been fortunate, and sometimes unfortunate, to experience many different types of leadership. Some leaders I encountered were brilliant tacticians or experts in their field, but they struggled to connect to the very people they were tasked with leading. Others weren't particularly gifted in the technical sense, but they had an uncanny ability to see people, to really see them, and in doing so, draw out more than anyone expected. Then there were those rare few who managed to balance both: technical mastery and human-centered care.

But here's what I found over time: no one leader had it all. There was no single style that worked in every situation, no blueprint that fit every person. The leaders I admired most, the ones I wanted to emulate, weren't those who tried to fit into a perfect mold. They were the ones who led with humility, adapted to the person or situation in front of them, listened with courage, and above all, showed empathy.

That's what this book is about.

It's not a manual. You won't find a set of guaranteed steps for becoming a great leader. I've sat through plenty of those kinds of trainings. I've read those books. While they have their place, I've learned that leadership can't be reduced to formulas. Leadership is too situational, too human, too unpredictable for that.

What I've offered here instead is reflection. It's a journey through moments, some big, some small, where I learned (often the hard way) what it means to lead with heart. Where I saw what happens when people feel safe enough to bring their truth to the table. Where I witnessed how the simple act of caring could change not just outcomes, but people themselves.

A powerful call to lead with empathy, presence, and courage. Real leadership begins not with authority, but with humanity.

I wrote this for all kinds of leaders:

For the person stepping into their very first supervisory role, wondering if they're ready.

For the seasoned leader who's lost touch with what inspired them to serve in the first place.

For the quiet contributor who doesn't have a title but leads every day in the way they treat others.

For anyone who's been handed authority and found themselves asking, "What do I do with this now?"

And for anyone who's ever wished their own leader had cared just a little bit more.

If there's one thread that runs through every page of this book, it's this: humans are at the center of everything we do. Lose sight of that, and no strategy, no process, no metric will save you. Keep that truth at the core of your leadership, and you will build trust that lasts. You will help people become more than they thought possible. Along the way, you will become more than you thought possible, too.

I hope as you read these pages, you'll see parts of your own journey reflected here—the doubts, the lessons, the quiet wins. I hope you'll feel encouraged not to chase perfection, but to pursue presence. To choose connection over command. To lead in a way that people will remember, not because of what you achieved, but because of how you made them feel along the way.

To lead, first be human. Only when people feel seen, heard, and valued will they give you their best and trust you with their truth.

Thank you for choosing to walk this road with me.

Introduction

The Quiet Reckoning

To Lead, First Be Human

Leadership books often begin with triumph. A lesson hard-won. A battle conquered. A defining moment where the author stood tall, earned the room's respect, and cemented their place as a leader worthy of your attention.

This book will not begin that way.

It begins instead with a decision I made that still unsettles me. A moment where I had the opportunity to show integrity, and I didn't. Not because I was malicious. Not because I lacked training. But because I wanted to win. Because I wanted to belong. Because I had just put on new stripes and hadn't yet figured out how to wear them with humility.

The event was simple, a squad competition during what we jokingly called "mandatory fun" in the Army. I had been asked to officiate one of the races, the kind of lighthearted event meant to build camaraderie and esprit de corps. One runner from my company crossed the finish line just behind the opponent. Barely a half-second difference. I saw it.

I knew it. But I called the race in favor of my own. Loyalty, right? Solidarity.

Wrong.

I was overruled by a superior, in my own company, no less. To this day, I don't know if that leader overruled me because they saw I called it wrong purposefully, or because they had simply seen what truly occurred and chose to call it correctly. I never asked. I only know what lived with me afterward.

It wasn't a reprimand. It wasn't a disciplinary action. It was the look on the other competitor's face. It was the small voice in the back of my mind that didn't raise its tone but refused to leave the room. It was the quiet shame of knowing I had missed an early opportunity to lead, not because I didn't have the stripes, but because I hadn't yet earned the weight of what they meant.

That was the beginning of something. Not of greatness. Not of a meteoric rise. But of a lifelong conversation I began having with myself: What does it actually mean to lead people?

This book is the continuation of that conversation.

Let me be clear from the start, I am not the leader this book describes. Not in full. No one is.

But I have met that leader. In glimpses. In fragments. In people who didn't even know they were showing me what leadership could be.

I've seen them in Command Sergeants who made coffee instead of barking orders. I've seen them in supervisors who professionally dismantled dismissive emails without raising their blood pressure or their voice.

I've seen them in teammates who challenged me with compassion, mentored me through mistakes, and reminded me that leadership isn't about being above, it's about being among.

What I've come to understand is this: leadership isn't one archetype. It isn't perfection in motion or wisdom personified. It isn't a checklist. It's a mosaic, a composite of characteristics, decisions, failures, recoveries, and intentions. We are not called to be the leader. We are called to become leaders, layer by layer, moment by moment, interaction by interaction.

This book is not written to preach. It is not designed to elevate me or anyone else to a pedestal that cannot and should not exist. Instead, it is an invitation.

An invitation to step away from titles.

To put down the myth of invincibility.

To abandon the idea that leadership is something you inherit with a promotion or acquire by osmosis.

This is a book about leadership as a psychological journey. A deeply human one.

It's about learning to listen before you speak, admit before you defend, and care before you calculate.

It's about the moments you wish you could take back, and the ones you hope to pass on.

It's for the new leader staring at the weight of a role they thought they were ready for. It's for the seasoned leader wondering if the pressure they feel means they're doing it wrong or doing it right.

And it's for anyone who has ever thought, *I'm not sure I'm built for this,* but showed up anyway.

You won't find commandments here. No "10 rules to greatness." No bullet-point prescriptions.

What you'll find are stories, some hard, some humbling, some quietly victorious, and reflections drawn from a lifetime of learning that leadership doesn't begin with knowing the answers. It begins with being willing to ask better questions.

So, consider this book your mirror. A place to see not just the leader you are, but the one you're becoming.

Welcome to the conversation.

Welcome to the reckoning.

Welcome to leadership, the human way.

Chapter 1
The Weight of a Title

Leadership doesn't come with a title. It's earned in the moments you choose integrity over ease.

I thought becoming a Sergeant would make me a leader. In the Army, "Sergeant" is a senior enlisted role, earned after years of following orders, now tasked with guiding a small team. The new stripes on my uniform felt like a badge of arrival. My boots shone brighter, my voice carried further, and suddenly people listened when I spoke. I stood taller, believing the title had transformed me.

I was wrong.

Weeks after my promotion, during a company "fun day," a lighthearted event to build team spirit, I faced my first real test. I was asked to officiate a squad race, a simple relay meant to spark camaraderie. One runner from my team crossed the finish line just behind the opponent, a half-second too late. I saw it clearly, but I called the race for my team.

Loyalty, I told myself. Solidarity.

It was a mistake.

A senior leader from my company overruled me. I don't know if they saw my intentional error or simply called it as they saw it. I never asked. What lingered was the quiet shame, the look on the other runner's face, the small voice in my head whispering I'd chosen image over integrity. That moment wasn't about losing a race. It was about missing a chance to lead.

This wasn't a career-ending failure, but it sparked a question I've carried ever since: What does it mean to earn the weight of a title, not just wear it?

The trap of a new title isn't unique to the military. Years later, during my graduate studies at Florida State University, I faced a similar temptation. As a requirement, I enrolled in a basic networking course, Networking 101, covering fundamentals like IP addressing and subnetting. For me, it felt like retaking the alphabet after writing novels. I was a Cisco Certified Network Associate for both data and voice, held a CompTIA Network+ certification, and had over 20 years of experience designing and troubleshooting enterprise networks across continents. I'd led response teams during outages and mentored junior technicians in environments far beyond the textbook.

When I saw the syllabus, I felt insulted—not by the material, but by the idea that my credentials didn't count. I wanted to raise my hand in class, list my certifications, and say, "I already know this." I was tempted to rely on my titles, the letters after my name, the years behind me, to be exempt, to skip the line.

But I didn't.

I sat with the discomfort, reminding myself that leadership isn't about proving what you know. It's about showing others how to carry themselves when no one's applauding. So, I leaned in. I asked thoughtful questions to spark discussion, stayed patient when classmates struggled, and never mentioned my certifications. Over time, peers learned of my expertise—not because I flaunted it, but because I helped them. When they asked how I knew so much, I shared humbly, without needing it to be the headline. That's when I realized: in civilian life, just like in uniform, leadership is earned through actions, not accolades.

Titles make you visible, but they can insulate you. They tempt you to take the easy route, to be liked, to win, to protect your image. I fell into that trap during the race, prioritizing my team's approval over fairness. In the classroom, I nearly did the same, craving recognition over contribution. Most new leaders face this temptation, whether it's fudging a deadline to impress a boss or avoiding a tough call to keep the peace. The real test isn't the title. It's what you do when no one's watching.

Another moment clarified this truth. Shortly after my promotion to Sergeant, I was tasked with leading a presentation on squad tactics—small-team strategies for field operations. The idea felt daunting. I'd executed these tactics as a soldier, but teaching them was different. I stood before my team, their eyes on me, expecting confidence. I remembered being in their seats, wondering if the leader had anything worth hearing. My nerves hummed, but my voice held steady.

What saved me wasn't memorized doctrine. It was the stories I shared, the mud of field training, the chaos of a missed radio call, the split-second fixes in real time. I wasn't just teaching tactics; I was translating experience. That's when I understood: leadership isn't about knowing more. It's about helping others make sense of what they know.

Years later, as a mid-level manager at the Department of State, I felt this lesson's echo. I led a team of seven seasoned professionals, assigning tasks in a high-stakes bureaucratic environment. When one team member accepted my decision without question, not because I outranked them, but because it made sense, I saw the shift. People don't follow titles. They follow clarity, judgment, and trust.

A title gets you into the room. Leadership earns you the right to stay. It's not about perfection but intention, owning mistakes, learning from them, and showing up for your people. When you stop pretending you've arrived, you start becoming a leader worth following.

Reflection: Earning Your Title

Leadership begins when you trade image for integrity. Pause and ask:

• Have you ever leaned on a title to avoid accountability? What happened?

• Are people following you because of your role or your presence?

• When you make decisions, are you trying to look right or get it right?

Action Step

Create a "Title Check" list. Write down three actions you can take this week to earn trust beyond your role—for example, admit a mistake, ask for feedback, or clarify a decision for your team. Revisit this list weekly to hold yourself accountable.

Chapter 2

The Power of Small Acts

No task is too small if it serves others. Humility in leadership starts with showing up where you're needed most.

The mess hall smelled of stale eggs and burnt toast, the kind of scent that clings to a room where soldiers shuffle through at dawn. Fluorescent lights buzzed overhead, casting a harsh glow on the linoleum floor, scuffed from years of boots. I stood by the coffee station, a battered machine that gurgled like it was on its last legs, my arms crossed and jaw tight.

I was a newly trained information systems specialist, fresh from six months of schooling on network design and internet security, ready to tackle routers and servers. Yet here I was, in my cavalry unit's executive section, assigned to the role of "administrations guy," shuffling papers, managing schedules, and, on this morning, making coffee.

The task stung. Coffee duty felt like a demotion, a chore for someone less skilled, less valuable. My hands hesitated over the grounds, my boots scuffed the floor in silent protest. I wasn't just brewing coffee; I was brewing resentment, convinced my training deserved better. Then the door creaked open, and the Sergeant Major stepped in.

A Sergeant Major is a unit's highest-ranking enlisted leader, a figure whose presence shifts the air, part mentor, part legend, all authority. His uniform was crisp, his boots polished, but his eyes carried the weight of years in the field. I braced for a critique, expecting him to call out my attitude. Instead, he walked to the coffee station, picked up the dented pot, and filled it with water from the sink. He scooped grounds into the filter, his movements deliberate, unhurried, as if brewing coffee was as vital as briefing a mission.

The machine hissed to life, and the rich, earthy scent began to cut through the mess hall's stale air. He didn't speak until the pot was full. Then, in a voice low but clear, he said, "Leadership isn't about being above the small stuff. It's about doing what keeps the team moving, even if it's just a cup of coffee."

His words didn't scold; they invited. They saw my frustration not as defiance but as a young soldier learning the ropes. I felt the knot in my chest loosen, replaced by a quiet clarity: no task is beneath a leader if it serves the mission.

That morning wasn't about coffee. It was about humility, leading through action, not ego. The Sergeant Major's simple act rewrote my understanding of service, showing me that trust is built in the unglamorous moments, when no one's watching.

This truth transcends the military. Years later, at the Department of State, I felt its echo in a server room that felt more like a bunker. The air was cold, a sterile chill engineered for machines, not people, leaving our fingers stiff and shoulders hunched. Cooling fans hummed, a relentless drone layered with the sporadic whir of spinning drives, drilling into our skulls after hours of troubleshooting.

Our team was deep in a systems upgrade, racing against a looming go-live date, battling glitches and bureaucratic pushback. Exhaustion wasn't just physical. It was bone-deep, the kind where your eyes burn and logic feels like chasing shadows.

Cables snaked across the floor, whiteboards were scrawled with frantic notes, and laptops flickered with command prompts. One colleague slumped in an office chair, elbows on a folding table, head in hands, still typing through a fog of surrender. We weren't frustrated anymore; we'd moved past that into a flat, quiet defeat, where effort outran hope. Then the door clicked open.

Our division director stepped in, his pressed shirt slightly rumpled, no tie, no entourage. He wasn't scheduled, wasn't expected. He carried a tray of foil-wrapped egg sandwiches and a stainless-steel carafe, steam curling from its spout. The smell of fresh coffee, warm and not the burnt sludge we'd nursed all night, cut through the room's stale air like a lifeline.

He set the tray down, poured himself a mug, and stood for a moment, his gaze steady, not judging the clutter but honoring the effort behind it.

"What's happening on the backend?" he asked, pulling up a chair, not at the table's head, but among us. For nearly an hour, he listened, nodding as we outlined dead ends and half solutions. His questions weren't a test; they were a bridge, drawing us back from isolation. He didn't offer fixes or platitudes. He just stayed, sharing the cold, the hum, the weight of the moment.

Those sandwiches, still warm, and that coffee didn't just feed us. They reminded us we were seen, that our late-night grind mattered.

Humility isn't confined to mess halls or server rooms. It's the teacher who scrubs paint off desks after an art project, unnoticed, so students can focus. It's the parent who folds laundry at midnight to ease a partner's load. These acts, small and often invisible, build trust because they say, *I'm here, and you matter.* They don't demand recognition; they create connection.

Leadership isn't about the spotlight. It's about seeing the work that needs doing and stepping into it, no matter how ordinary. When you lead with humility, you give others permission to do the same. That's when trust takes root, not in titles or triumphs, but in the quiet moments where you choose others over ego.

Reflection: The Strength in Small Acts

Humility forges trust through service. Pause and ask:

- When have you dismissed a task as "beneath" you? How did it affect those around you?

- Who has earned your trust with a quiet, selfless act? What made it unforgettable?

- What small act can you do today to show up for your team, family, or community?

Action Step

Build a "Humble Acts" journal. For one week, record one small, selfless task you do each day to support others—for example, tidying a shared space, listening without interrupting, or helping with a minor chore. Note how these acts shift trust or morale, for you and those around you. Revisit your journal to reflect on patterns and impact.

Chapter 3
Leaders are Made, Not Born

Leadership isn't a gift you're born with. It's a skill you build, one faltering step at a time, through persistence and practice.

I used to believe leaders were a different breed—charismatic, fearless, born to command a room. Early in my Army career, I learned how wrong I was. As a young specialist in a signal unit, responsible for maintaining communication networks, I was tasked with delivering a briefing on our system's readiness to a room of senior officers. A "bricfing" in the military is a high-stakes presentation where clarity and confidence are non-negotiable, and every word lands under scrutiny.

The thought of it turned my stomach. Public speaking wasn't my strength. My voice cracked under pressure, my hands shook, and my mind raced with worst-case scenarios: stumbling over terms like "bandwidth" or "encryption," or worse, blanking entirely. The night before, I paced my barracks room, its cinderblock walls closing in under the hum of a flickering fluorescent light. I rehearsed in front of a cracked mirror, my reflection a mix of determination and dread, tripping over slides I'd memorized but couldn't deliver smoothly.

When the moment came, I stood at the front of the conference room, the air thick with the scent of stale coffee and polished brass. Officers' eyes fixed on me, their notepads open, pens poised. My throat tightened, but I started. My voice wavered at first, thin against the room's silence. I fumbled a slide transition, my fingers clumsy on the clicker. But I kept going, leaning on the hours of practice, the notes scribbled in margins, the feedback from a mentor who'd told me, "It's not about perfection. It's about showing up."

By the end, I wasn't polished, but I was clear. The officers nodded, asked questions, and I answered—not flawlessly, but honestly. Sweat beaded on my forehead, but a quiet relief settled in my chest. I hadn't been born to brief rooms. I'd learned to do it, one shaky step at a time. That day taught me: leadership isn't innate. It's forged in the moments you push past fear and keep trying.

This lesson isn't just for military briefings. Years later, as a non-traditional undergraduate student, I felt it echo in a college classroom. I wasn't the typical student, fresh from high school and living in dorms. I was in federal service, juggling a full-time job, bills, and deadlines that didn't pause for exams. My apartment's kitchen table, lit by the glow of a second-hand laptop, was my study hall, where instant coffee fueled late-night cramming. I was on my own, no spouse, no kids, just me proving to myself I could finish what I'd started.

In a business communications class, I was assigned to a group project: a presentation analyzing a case study on team dynamics. The task sounded straightforward, but group work rarely is. Our first meeting was a mess—missed deadlines, half-baked ideas, an outline that looked like a rushed Google search. The classroom, with its squeaky chairs and faint smell of dry-erase markers, buzzed with other groups' chatter, but ours sat in uneasy silence. I stayed quiet at first, not wanting to seem overbearing as the older student. But as weeks passed and chaos grew, I saw a choice: stay silent and scrape by or step up and steer.

I chose to steer. Not with a lecture, but with a quiet offer: "How about I draft a framework we can build from?" That night, I worked at my kitchen table, the clock ticking past midnight, mapping slides and assigning roles based on my teammates' strengths—one confident speaker, one visual whiz, one shy but diligent researcher.

The next meeting, in a cramped library study room, felt different. The fog lifted. The quiet teammate volunteered to open the presentation, her voice tentative but resolute. We found a rhythm, a shared purpose.

Our delivery wasn't flawless. Slides lagged; voices shook. But it was unified, proud, alive with effort. We earned one of the highest grades in the class. Afterward, a teammate pulled me aside in the hallway, her backpack slung over one shoulder. "I almost dropped this course," she said. "This project made it worth staying."

Her words landed like a gift, not praise, but proof that leadership isn't about being the loudest. It's about building a bridge for others to cross.

Leadership isn't a birthright. It's the teacher who practices tough conversations with a struggling student until they land right. It's the coworker who refines a pitch through late-night revisions to lift the team. These skills—clarity, courage, structure—aren't gifts. They're earned through persistence, failure, and practice. No one is born to lead. We become leaders by choosing to grow, one small, unsteady step at a time.

Reflection: Growing into Leadership

Leadership is a skill, not a talent. Pause and ask:

• What leadership skill have you struggled with? How did you work to improve it?

• Who has modeled growth in leadership for you? What did their effort look like?

• What small step can you take this week to practice a leadership skill?

Action Step

Create a "Growth Steps" plan. Identify one leadership skill you want to develop (for example, public speaking, organizing teams, giving feedback). List three small actions to practice it this week, such as rehearsing a presentation, drafting a team agenda, or asking for feedback on a decision. Track your progress and note how each step builds confidence.

Chapter 4

Leading through resistance

Leadership doesn't demand authority. It builds influence through relationships, one conversation at a time.

Bureaucracy isn't just red tape. It's a shrug, a stalled email, a quiet "this is how it's always been." Sometimes, it's the face of someone who could help but won't. Leadership means pushing through those cracks, not with force but with persistence, relationships, and a touch of audacity.

In South Korea, on a sprawling U.S. military base thick with dust and diesel, I faced bureaucracy's stubborn heart. As a civilian with the Department of Defense, I inherited 67 data lines—digital lifelines for joint U.S.-Korean operations. These weren't just internet cables; they were the backbone of a global defense network, neglected for over 15 years, undocumented, insecure, limping along. My job was to accredit each one, verifying cybersecurity, updating systems, and rooting out rogue devices. Picture driving across miles of base, knocking on doors, explaining to skeptical strangers why their forgotten networks needed scrutiny.

Most cooperated, especially Korean IT staff who grasped the stakes. But at one site, I hit a wall. A Korean technician, his eyes wary under a fluorescent glare, guarded four of those 67 lines. His server room, a dusty bunker humming with overheating equipment, felt like a fortress. "Not feasible," he said, citing bandwidth limits and protocols, his tone flat. My DoD badge meant nothing; he answered to his American supervisor, a lanky officer with a sharp drawl and a desk buried in reports.

I escalated, expecting an ally. Instead, the supervisor dismissed me: "It's been fine for years. Why fix what's unbroken?" His shrug was bureaucracy incarnate—slow, silent inertia.

Frustration burned, the weight of deadlines pressing like the room's stale air. I could have walked away, filed a report, and let the system grind on. But those four lines were critical, and every day they stayed unaccredited, the network grew weaker. So, I did the unthinkable: I made it broken.

I contacted the peninsula's central IT authority and requested a four-hour suspension of those circuits—just enough to jolt the system without lasting harm. The base noticed. Phones rang. Work stalled.

The supervisor roared into my office, six miles across the base, his face flushed. "What the hell are you doing?" he demanded. I didn't flinch. I laid out my evidence—emails, logs, warnings I'd sent for weeks, ignored. I showed him his systems' decay: expired machines, security gaps, inefficiencies dragging his team down. The fight drained from him, replaced by a flicker of respect. He saw not an outsider but someone who cared enough to risk the fight. He ordered his technician to cooperate fully.

It took five months—hunting devices in closets, replacing obsolete gear, documenting every wire—but we accredited those four lines, and the 67-line project hummed. The supervisor's team thrived, morale soared, and he earned a commendation, complete with a bonus. We became friends. I didn't need the ribbon; I needed the system to work. Sometimes, leadership means being the villain in Act One so someone else can shine in Act Three.

This lesson carried to Paris, at a U.S. embassy pulsing with diplomatic stakes. As a midlevel officer, I faced a subtler resistance. The mailroom supervisor, a steady worker with a quiet command, was undermined by an outside liaison who doubted his competence.

The embassy's marble halls, cool and echoing, hid the mailroom's chaos—packages stacked high, the sharp scent of ink cutting through ringing phones. The liaison, a sharp-eyed woman I knew casually, bypassed the supervisor, tasking his subordinate directly via email, eroding his authority.

In government, respect isn't just courtesy; it's operational glue. The supervisor's frustration simmered, trust fraying. I could have ignored it, but cracks like these deepen into dysfunction. I met the liaison privately, not with anger but curiosity. Why the bypass? What was at stake?

In a cramped lounge, its air heavy with burnt coffee, she admitted doubting the supervisor's speed. I clarified the boundary: tasking goes through him, not around him. "If you see a gap," I said, "escalate with context, and trust supervision to act." I followed up with an email, copied to all but the subordinate, affirming her insight but reinforcing the chain. The air cleared, the supervisor stood taller, and trust held.

This truth isn't confined to bases or embassies. At the Department of State, as a new midlevel leader, I met resistance from Mike, a team lead whose expertise outstripped my own. The office, a gray cubicle maze under flickering lights, hummed with keyboards and printers. Mike's emails were curt, his replies clipped: "not feasible" mid-sentence. His decade of mastery—networks, shortcuts—made my title irrelevant.

I walked to his office, past beige cabinets, and asked, "What's a fix you've done that no one noticed?" He shared a network redundancy tweak that saved hours, unthanked. I listened, gave him credit in a team meeting, and kept showing up—asking, learning his priorities. When a project loomed, I asked what he could tackle fastest. He delivered, not for my title but for our trust.

Leadership isn't muscling through. It's finesse—knowing when to disrupt, when to pause, when to hold the center. It's the coworker who learns a teammate's needs to align a project. It's the organizer who asks a neighbor's input before a community drive. Bureaucracy will always drag, but leaders keep showing up with duct tape, dignity, and a steady hand.

Reflection: Navigating Resistance

Leadership in stalled systems demands persistence. Ask:
- When have you faced bureaucratic inertia? How did you push through?
- Who has earned your trust by respecting structure? What did they do?
- What small act can you take today to bridge resistance with respect?

Action Step

Create a *Navigate Resistance* plan. Identify a bureaucratic hurdle you face. List three actions to address it this week, such as building rapport with a gatekeeper, clarifying a boundary, or escalating with evidence. Track progress and note shifts in resistance.

Chapter 5

People Are the Mission

Lead the work, but serve the people.

If you spend enough time in government, military, or technical leadership roles, something insidious starts to happen.

You begin to confuse the work with the people.

The deliverables become more urgent than the humans behind them.

The dashboards matter more than the eyes staring back at you in the team meeting.

And little by little, tasks start to feel more real than trust.

I've fallen into that trap. I think most people have.

Because the metrics are always easier to measure than morale.

The spreadsheet shows up on time. The silent burnout does not.

But what I've come to learn, through missteps, hard conversations, and some humbling moments, is that people are not the means to the mission. People are the mission. If you lead long enough, the lesson becomes impossible to ignore.

I didn't learn this in a single moment. I learned it over years, through practice and presence.

I remember being a mid-level manager with the Department of State, assigned to a team of seven. These were seasoned professionals. Not fresh hires. Not rookies. Grown men and women, many of them older than me, most of them highly competent in their own right.

And I had been given the responsibility to direct their daily efforts.

At first, I approached the job the way most new leaders do—with efficiency in mind. I delegated. I monitored. I assigned tasks like I was assembling a puzzle. But over time, I began to realize that the puzzle wasn't just about workload. It was about fit. About energy. About who felt seen, who felt sidelined, and who brought more to the table when they were given work that meant something to them.

That's when I started to do things differently.

I began to ask not just, "Can you do this?" but, "Do you want to?"

Not just, "Is this within your scope?" but, "Does this align with your strengths?"

That wasn't just about kindness. It was about performance.

Because when people feel personally invested, they don't just comply. They contribute.

Recognition became my greatest tool—not rewards, not reprimands, not rigid oversight.

And not just the loud, public kind of recognition either, though there's a place for that. Sometimes the most powerful thing you can do for someone is notice something quiet and say so.

"I saw the way you handled that difficult customer. That was grace under pressure."

"You've been carrying more than your share of the backend tasks lately. I appreciate that."

"The way you jumped in without being asked? That matters."

These aren't grand speeches. They're moments.

But they accumulate. They embed. And they do something that memos never will: they make people feel seen.

I saw this principle come alive in the middle of a highly technical, high-stakes project. Our parent IT organization was flattening and simplifying the structure of our Active Directory domain—a digital directory service that essentially controls who can access what across a government enterprise. At the time, our domain was buried three tiers deep from the root, needlessly complex, cumbersome, and full of legacy handoffs no one fully owned anymore.

It wasn't just bureaucratic cleanup.

It had real-world consequences for how we, as a team, interacted with our clients every single day.

And yet, no one had spoken to us about how this would work. Not a meeting. Not a briefing. Not even a courtesy email to the Tier 3 arm of our IT team, where some of our most talented staff lived.

So we looked into it ourselves.

We met. We dissected the changes. We asked the hard questions.

And one team member usually quiet, sometimes reserved spoke up with a kind of clarity and conviction that stopped the room. This wasn't just annoyance or curiosity. It was investment.

He saw the flaws. He saw the risk.

And more importantly, he saw the solution.

I made the easiest leadership decision of the month: I got out of the way.

I gave him full responsibility to align our section's interests with the broader Active Directory overhaul. And he didn't just carry the task. He transformed it.

He worked behind the scenes to resolve every inconsistency the other team left behind. He patched their gaps, smoothed their assumptions, and documented what they missed. And he did it with excellence not because anyone told him to, but because someone trusted him to.

After the project wrapped, he pulled me aside not to complain, not to ask for recognition, but to thank me for assigning him the work.

Let that sink in.

He thanked me for the opportunity to carry a burden.

Because to him, it wasn't just a burden. It was a chance to operate in purpose.

That experience reshaped how I led from then on.

When you align someone's strength with the task at hand, they don't just deliver the work. They invest in the outcome.

They don't just check boxes. They elevate the standard.

And the rest of the team sees it not just the result, but the reason behind it.

From that point on, I made it my mission to spot alignment opportunities early.

If someone fell short in skill, I didn't sideline them. I resourced them. I paired them with someone who could teach. I offered them training. I reframed the task as a growth path instead of a test.

Because that's what leaders do when they understand this truth:

The mission matters. But the people delivering it will always matter more.

Reflection: The People Behind the Work

Leadership isn't about keeping the trains running on time.

It's about knowing who's on board and why they're riding in the first place.

So, ask yourself:

- Are you managing deliverables, or are you developing people?
- Are your team members performing, or are they invested?
- And when someone struggles, do you write them off, or ask what resource, coaching, or context they might need to rise?

Because here's the quiet truth of leadership:

People aren't just your greatest asset. They're your entire strategy.

And if you take care of them with clarity, compassion, and trust, they'll move mountains.

But if you treat them like interchangeable parts, you'll always be rebuilding what they never had the reason to build with you.

People are not the means.

They are the mission.

And the best leaders never forget it.

Chapter 6

The Lie of the All-Knowing Leader

Real leadership isn't about always knowing. It's about never pretending.

There's a particular pressure that comes with leadership, one that doesn't show up on paper.

It's the pressure to know. To have the answer. To be the answer.

It creeps in quietly.

People start looking at you a little differently. They wait for your cue in meetings. They expect your signature on the plan. They glance in your direction when something goes wrong.

And it doesn't matter how collaborative you claim to be, sooner or later, you start to feel like you're only as good as your last right answer.

It's one of the most destructive myths in leadership: that good leaders know everything, and great ones never show weakness.

This myth is subtle, but powerful. It doesn't usually start with arrogance. It starts with expectation, real or imagined. And if you let it, it will warp your leadership from thoughtful to performative, from human to hollow.

I remember a moment when this myth collided head-on with reality.

I was stationed at the U.S. Embassy in Paris. Our team had submitted a request to the regional support center, a group responsible for helping missions like ours with highly specialized technical tasks.

This request wasn't simple. It dealt with radio configurations, the kind of work that sits at the intersection of legacy hardware and mission-critical communications. No one on our team was an expert in it. Not me. Not the person writing the request. Not the backup support.

And that's why we reached out.

We weren't asking for a handout. We were doing what responsible teams do: seeking help when the task exceeded our capabilities.

The response we received was juvenile. It wasn't just dismissive. It was borderline mocking.

Comments like "We can come there and show you how to do this" weren't just unhelpful. They were unprofessional. The kind of response that wraps condescension in the language of assistance. The kind that says, *We're not really here to help. We're here to remind you that you should have known this already.*

But here's the part that stuck with me.

The email didn't come to me. It came to someone else, a leader I deeply admired.

And he responded—swiftly, directly, and professionally.

He didn't raise his voice. He didn't lose composure. But he did dismantle the tone. He did point out the disrespect. And he did reassert the seriousness of the request, the credibility of our team, and the expectation that support be given without ridicule.

That email was more than a rebuttal. It was a shield.

He didn't need to prove he knew radio configurations. He needed to prove that we were worth backing up, even when we didn't.

That's what leadership looks like when it's not about knowing. It's about covering, protecting, and standing up in the gap between the problem and your people.

When the email hit our inboxes, the energy on the team shifted.

We felt seen.

We felt defended.

And more than anything, we felt safe, because we had a leader who wasn't pretending to be an expert. He was being present when it counted.

That Paris email wasn't the only time I saw leadership sharpen itself in the absence of certainty.

Not long before that, when I was working for the Department of the Army, I found myself dropped into an entirely unfamiliar role, responsible for managing the underground cable systems that supported digital communications across the entire installation.

The person who had been in charge left abruptly. And the job, complex, technical, and invisible to most, still needed doing.

I had never worked in that space before. I had no experience managing wiring infrastructure, much less underground pathways or network diagrams that spanned multiple buildings. But I didn't panic.

Instead, I did what I've learned to do when thrown into something new: I started listening. I started asking. And I stayed honest about what I didn't know.

I walked the grounds. I met with engineers. I stared at maps until they stopped looking like spaghetti and started resembling strategy. Bit by bit, I got my footing.

And then came the challenge: a high-stakes meeting where a department lead announced they needed 125 computers and 300 phone lines relocated across campus in two weeks.

I could've nodded. I could've smiled and said "we'll try." But I didn't.

I laid out the facts. Not as a protest, but as a professional.

I explained that a move like that required planning, surveys, materials, and design work, none of which could realistically be done in 14 days. Even the team responsible for the work required two weeks just to evaluate the site before giving a quote.

The room quieted. Then something surprising happened.

They listened.

The project was pushed back six months. Not because I gave them what they wanted, but because I gave them what was real.

Later, I learned my predecessor had tried to make the same case, but couldn't quite convey the complexity in a way leadership could absorb. The difference wasn't in my expertise. It was in my posture.

I had taken the time to learn, not just the task, but the context. I had built relationships. I had been honest about what I didn't know, and diligent in learning it.

That transparency became my credibility. And that credibility became my influence.

That's the real myth of the all-knowing leader: not just that we're supposed to know everything, but that admitting we don't somehow weakens us.

In reality, the opposite is true.

The leaders who are most respected aren't the ones with the fastest answers. They're the ones with the deepest trust, because they have nothing to hide.

Because they're willing to pause. To ask. To say: "I'm not sure, but I will find out."

That's not weakness. That's strength in its most grounded form.

Reflection — When You Don't Know

You will be asked questions you don't know the answers to. You will be placed in roles where you are not the expert. And you will be expected to lead through ambiguity.

The myth says that when this happens, you fake it. The truth is that when this happens, you lean in.

So, ask yourself:

• Are you pretending to be confident, or are you building confidence through learning?

• Do your team members believe you always have the answer, or do they know you'll always tell them the truth?

• And when uncertainty shows up, do you treat it like a threat, or like an opportunity to grow?

Because leadership isn't about having all the answers. It's about holding the space until better answers appear, and making sure no one gets steamrolled in the meantime.

You don't have to be all-knowing. You just have to be all-in.

Curious. Honest. Accountable. Human.

Because that's what your team needs. And more often than not, it's what makes them believe in you—even when you're still finding your way.

Chapter 7

Emotional Labor is Real Work

Leadership isn't just mental. It's emotional.

There's a kind of work that doesn't show up on timecards.

No spreadsheet tracks it. No award recognizes it. And few people even talk about it openly.

But it's there. Every day. In every meeting. In every moment when you're not just guiding a task, you're managing energy.

You're monitoring who's disengaged, who's carrying too much, who's not being heard. You're deciding when to step in, when to hold back, when to defuse tension, and when to sit quietly so someone else can be heard—even when you're exhausted.

That's not administrative labor.

That's not management. That's emotional labor.

And if you're leading people, not projects, not spreadsheets, not systems, then emotional labor is your full-time job.

Early in my career, I thought leadership was about what you could do.

The decisions you made. The work you produced. The knowledge you carried.

But the more I led teams, the more I realized leadership wasn't just about deliverables. It was about emotional stewardship.

The unspoken part of the job is that you become a kind of thermostat for the team's emotional climate.

If you're rattled, they feel it. If you're distant, they withdraw. If you're dismissive, they shut down.

But if you're present, truly present, they don't just work harder. They trust deeper.

This is the part of leadership no one trains you for.

There's no manual for sensing a team member is off their game.

No checklist for intuiting that someone's silence in a meeting isn't about disinterest, but fear.

No course module for holding space when someone is spiraling because of something that's not on the agenda, but is very much in the room.

And yet, if you ignore these things, everything else suffers.

Because people don't leave jobs.

They leave environments that make them feel invisible.

I didn't come to understand this overnight.

It took me years, and one especially pivotal tool, to see just how differently people carry and express conflict.

That tool was the Thomas-Kilmann Conflict Mode Instrument, or TKI.

At its surface, it's a framework, a simple way of classifying conflict styles:

- Competing
- Collaborating
- Compromising
- Avoiding
- Accommodating

But what it did for me went far beyond categories.

It gave me language for emotional awareness—both mine and others'.

It made me realize that people aren't difficult. They're just different.

And if you treat every conflict like it's a debate to be won, you'll lose your team long before you win the point.

In my early years in the military, emotional nuance wasn't a leadership priority.

We didn't ask, "How are you feeling today?"

We asked, "Are you motivated?"

And we didn't say it gently. We barked it. We shouted it like a challenge. Because in a combat environment, hesitation can cost lives, and no one's going to ask if it's a good time to get shot at.

The absurdity of that question in that context still makes me laugh.

But here's the thing: not every mission is combat.

And when you leave the battlefield and enter the boardroom, the briefing room, or the daily grind of civilian leadership, that same "do it because I said so" posture doesn't just fall flat. It causes real damage.

I learned that the hard way.

I once had a team member under my supervision—sharp, respectful, always agreeable. Culturally different from me, but committed to doing the work.

Any time I gave him a task, his response was the same:

"On it."

Short. Direct. Respectful. Everything I had once been trained to value.

But the deliverables told a different story.

There were gaps. Revisions. Misunderstandings.

And over time, those small cracks turned into lost days, then lost weeks. We were misfiring, and I didn't know why.

At first, I assumed the issue was follow-through. Maybe he wasn't listening carefully. But the truth was more complicated, and more humbling.

He wasn't disagreeing. He was accommodating.

Which, according to the Thomas-Kilmann Conflict Mode Instrument, is one of the five conflict responses people use to navigate tension or uncertainty.

An *accommodator* avoids conflict by going along with what's asked—even when they don't fully understand, don't agree, or need clarification. It's not about laziness or incompetence. It's about respect. Deference. Sometimes fear. Sometimes shame.

And in this case, it was about face—the unspoken cultural imperative to avoid embarrassment at all costs.

He wasn't defiant.

He was being polite.

But my "directness" didn't land as clarity. It landed as pressure.

And every "on it" was his way of buying time, not signaling confidence.

Once I saw that, once I understood his style, everything changed.

I stopped delivering tasks like marching orders and started opening conversations.

"Walk me through how you'd approach this."

"What's unclear or needs more context?"

"Let's talk through your first steps so we're aligned."

The difference was immediate.

Fewer revisions. More ownership.

And a working relationship built on mutual understanding, not just mutual respect.

That was the moment I realized what emotional labor really is.

It's not just managing feelings. It's interpreting unspoken language. It's translating leadership into the dialect your team can hear.

The tools we use in battle—command, compliance, control—don't translate to human-centered leadership.

Not in the long term.

Not if you want people to follow you with belief, not just obedience.

It's not enough to issue clear directives.

You have to notice how they land.

You have to understand the difference between silence and agreement, between "I'm fine" and "I'm overwhelmed," between "on it" and ready.

Because in leadership, what's unsaid is often what matters most.

Reflection — The Cost of Emotional Blindness

Leadership isn't just logic. It's emotional translation.

It's the ability to read the tension beneath someone's nod.

To hear the fatigue in someone's voice before they name it.

To adjust, not because you're soft, but because you're skilled.

So ask yourself:

• Are you leading people in the way you prefer to communicate, or in the way they can receive?

• When a team member seems disengaged, do you interpret it as laziness, or explore it as disconnection?

• Are you treating emotional awareness like a side job, or like the actual job?

Because here's the truth:

Emotional labor is not soft work. It is leadership work.

And the ones who do it well don't burn out. They build trust.

Not by pretending to have every answer.

But by paying attention to every signal.

And speaking to people, not at them, in a language their head and heart can both understand.

That's not a footnote in leadership. That's the foundation.

Chapter 8

The Cost of the Role

The more you carry others, the more you need to protect what's left of yourself.

Most people who step into leadership think the cost will be time.

Late nights. Overflowing inboxes. Weekend meetings that weren't supposed to happen.

And yes, time is part of it. But it's rarely the most expensive thing leadership asks of you.

The real cost is emotional real estate.

The mental energy you expend anticipating needs, reading the room, writing the careful message, choosing the right moment to correct or encourage, or simply not respond because you know the weight of your words isn't casual anymore.

The real cost is presence, how often you're physically with your family but mentally processing what went wrong in the meeting five hours earlier.

The real cost is joy, the subtle dulling of enthusiasm because leadership is no longer a challenge. It's an identity. One you wear so tightly you forget what it feels like to not be the person others rely on.

Leadership, if left unchecked, doesn't just take time. It takes you.

I've felt that pull more than once.

There were weeks when I gave everything I had to the team. I showed up early, answered questions patiently, resolved conflict, redirected tasks, and filled in gaps. And then I'd get home and realize I had nothing left for the people who matter most.

I'd stare blankly through dinner. I'd answer my spouse with "one second" while replying to one more message. I'd sit on the couch but not actually be there.

Not because I didn't care. But because I had run out of myself.

And that's the part no one warns you about.

They say leadership is service. They don't say that service can hollow you out from the inside if you're not careful.

One of the moments that shook me happened when I had submitted an important work product to my supervisor, something my team had poured themselves into. It had taken time. Late hours. Collective effort.

The response came back swiftly.

"It is inadequate. Do more."

No context. No feedback. No direction. Just three words: Do more.

I was crestfallen. Not because my ego was bruised. I've long since learned to hold criticism without letting it shape my worth.

What got to me was different.

It was my team I couldn't stop thinking about.

They had already done more. They had bent their schedules. Stayed late. Asked smart questions. Checked every box.

And now I had to return to them, not just with a rejection, but with no explanation.

I sat with that for longer than I'd like to admit. I sat with it through the end of the workday. I carried it home.

And that's when I felt the cost, not in the meeting room, but in my living room.

My kids were trying to tell me about their favorite ride at Six Flags or the new playground slide they had conquered, and I was nodding but not really hearing them. I was in the room, but I wasn't present.

My wife noticed before I did. She looked me in the eye and said, "You need to do whatever needs doing to find your center. Focus on what's important."

She wasn't accusing me. She was inviting me, inviting me to come back to myself.

The next morning, I took a deep breath and did something that's deceptively hard in many hierarchies: I went back to my supervisor.

I wasn't combative. I wasn't emotional. I simply said, "If I'm going to ask my team to do more, again, I need something more to give them. I need substance. I need direction. I need a target."

To their credit, my supervisor responded with generosity. They didn't double down. They didn't make it personal. Instead, they gave me a thoughtful, three-paragraph synopsis outlining what was strong about our submission, where it missed the mark, and how we could close the gap.

That document changed everything.

Because I knew my team. I knew how to translate feedback into fuel. And this time, I had enough fuel to light the right fire.

I rewrote the expectations in terms that matched their strengths. I paired the stretch goals with context.

And when they delivered, they delivered. The final product exceeded every expectation. It didn't just check boxes. It stunned.

Even better, it changed the way my supervisor responded in the future.

No more one-line dismissals. They saw that feedback isn't a courtesy, it's a leadership tool. One that requires effort and respect.

Not just because teams deserve direction. But because when people give their all, they deserve to feel seen.

That experience taught me something I wish more leaders understood.

The emotional cost of leadership isn't just what you feel. It's what you absorb.

You take the hit so your team doesn't have to. You hold the frustration. You rewrite the message. You ask for clarity.

And if you're not careful, you burn out, not from overwork, but from over-carrying.

Leadership is not martyrdom. But it often comes with silence.

No one sees you shielding your team from political pressure. No one claps when you rewrite someone's failure into a growth opportunity. No one cheers when you're up at night, not because of deadlines, but because you don't want to break the spirit of someone who's already doing their best.

This is the part of leadership no title captures.

Reflection – What Are You Carrying?

No one talks about the grief of leadership.

The little losses. The missed dinners. The words left unspoken because you were still rehearsing the right tone to say it in.

So, ask yourself:

- Are you measuring your leadership by output alone, or by the weight you're carrying that no one sees?
- Are you present at home, or are you still trying to solve work in your head while nodding through bedtime stories?
- Are you giving your team clarity and care, but giving yourself none?

Because here's the truth:

Leadership asks for everything. But you are not required to give it your entire self.

You are allowed to push back.

You are allowed to say, "That feedback isn't enough. My team deserves better." You are allowed to leave work at work and still be a damn good leader.

And most importantly? You are allowed to be whole.

Chapter 9

The Greatest Lie We Tell Ourselves

Leadership was never about domination. That was the myth. The truth is, care moves faster than control ever could.

There's a lie we whisper to ourselves when the stakes are high and the pressure is rising.

A lie dressed in confidence.

A lie reinforced by outdated management playbooks, boot camp memories, and a thousand bad bosses who confused fear for respect.

The lie goes like this:

"If I want it done right, I need to control everything." Or worse:

"If I don't assert my power, they'll stop listening."

That lie has teeth.

It feeds on anxiety and self-doubt. It masquerades as strength. And if you believe it, truly believe it, it will convince you that being "in charge" means always being in control.

But here's the truth that too few people say out loud:

Control doesn't scale. It burns out leaders and it boxes in teams.

The more you grip, the less anyone can breathe.

The more you demand obedience, the less you get buy-in.

And slowly, something corrosive happens.

People stop bringing you their truth.

They stop offering new ideas.

They do the task, but they don't bring their heart with them.

They comply, but they don't care.

And that's the fastest way to kill a mission, from the inside out.

The lie of domination is especially tempting when your reputation is on the line, when someone above you wants results yesterday, and someone below you just made a mistake you'll have to answer for.

In those moments, barking orders feels efficient.

But it's emotional debt.

You might save five minutes now, but you'll spend five weeks later repairing the trust you broke.

I've seen it. I've done it. I've caught myself gripping too tightly not because I was confident, but because I was scared to fall.

But time and again, I've learned that the real antidote to chaos isn't dominance. It's clarity and care.

You don't move faster by pushing people harder.

You move faster when people want to help you win.

And people don't want to win with someone who makes them feel replaceable.

I once worked for a leader who, to this day, defines what micromanagement looks like in its most aggressive form.

Every task, big or small, came with constant hovering. Not thoughtful oversight. Not engaged support. Just relentless involvement. At first, I chalked it up to the learning curve of a new assignment, or the pressure of high-stakes projects. But over time, it became clear. This was his way. This was his definition of leadership.

He didn't want the task done right. He wanted it done his way.

At first, I was frustrated. Then I was confused. Eventually, I started to second-guess myself. Even when he gave praise, it felt off, as though he was applauding himself for managing me so closely rather than recognizing the work I had done.

One day, I'd had enough. I pulled him aside, quietly and privately, and asked him, "Do you think I'm doing a decent job?"

He didn't hesitate. "You're doing an outstanding job."

And from somewhere deep inside, the words rose before I could even think to stop them.

"Then back off."

To his credit, he did, with me anyway. But not with the others.

I watched him burn out in slow motion, trying to be manager, worker, architect, and executor all at once. He believed his value came from doing, not from developing. He thought leadership meant carrying the entire load rather than building people up to share it.

He confused perfection with effectiveness.

And in doing so, he lost the trust of his team and eventually the energy to carry even himself.

Micromanagement doesn't just smother progress. It distorts potential.

It's not just exhausting.

It's erasure.

A slow dismantling of confidence that leaves people unsure of what they're actually capable of.

Compare that to another leader I had. She wasn't loud. She didn't hover. She didn't feel the need to be in every room or comment on every move. But when she spoke, you listened, not out of obligation but out of respect.

She gave space.

She gave clarity.

And most importantly, she gave trust.

When she handed me a complex, cross-functional project, something I'd never formally led before, she didn't insert herself into every step. She simply asked, "Do you need anything from me to succeed?" Then she stepped back.

I wasn't sure at first. The task felt big. The moving parts were many. I hadn't yet led across silos. But the way she framed the work, breaking it down into something understandable and winnable, made it feel like something I could rise to. And so, I did.

And here's what made the difference.

It wasn't her instructions that carried me through. It was her belief.

That belief translated into confidence.

That confidence translated into action.

And that action, in turn, earned the respect of every team I coordinated with.

When the project wrapped, she surprised me with an award. Not just publicly, but quietly she pulled me aside and said, "I'm proud of what you did."

That moment still lives with me. Not because of the praise, but because she embodied the kind of leadership that multiplies capacity rather than measuring it.

She didn't just assign the task. She assigned ownership.

She didn't dictate outcomes. She nurtured growth.

She didn't need control. She modeled trust.

And so, here's the truth.

The greatest lie we tell ourselves in leadership is that control equals effectiveness.

It doesn't.

Control might feel like strength, but it's fueled by fear, fear of being questioned, of being outshined, of not knowing something.

Trust, on the other hand, is fueled by courage. And it takes real courage to say:

"I see something in you. Go make it happen."

Dominance demands obedience. Belief inspires growth.

One will drain your team and leave you standing alone.

The other will build a team that can stand with you, stronger, more resilient, and more capable than you could ever be on your own.

At the end of the day, the choice is simple.

You can grip tighter. Or you can grow leaders.

But you can't do both.

Reflection — Letting Go to Lift Others

If leadership were just about knowing the most or doing the most, then the most controlling leaders would be the most effective. But we both know they're not.

Leadership isn't about having the tightest grip. It's about knowing when to loosen it.

It's easy to believe that your value comes from being in every decision, every detail. But real leadership isn't about being in the middle of everything. It's about building people who can move things forward when you're not there.

So, take a moment. Ask yourself:

- Do people bring you their best because they're inspired, or because they're afraid to disappoint you?
- Are you building a team that relies on your presence, or one that carries forward your trust?
- Are you leading like a gatekeeper, or like a gardener creating the conditions for others to grow?

The leaders we remember aren't the ones who hovered the most. They're the ones who stood back just far enough to let us rise.

The ones who gave us responsibility before we thought we were ready.

The ones who stayed close enough to catch us, but distant enough to let us learn.

The ones who believed in us, clearly, boldly, and without micromanaging every step.

That's what real authority looks like. Not control. Not ego.

Just belief, well placed and freely given.

And that kind of belief doesn't diminish your power.

It multiplies it.

Chapter 10

Leadership Is a Human Undertaking

The real work of leadership was never strategic. It was always personal.

There's a truth we quietly resist, especially those of us trained in tactics, sharpened by systems, or conditioned by crisis. A truth that feels almost too soft to admit in the rooms where decisions are made.

It goes like this:

Leadership is emotional labor.

Not just strategy. Not just coordination. Real leadership is about how you hold space for people. How you carry their doubt alongside your own. How you make someone feel when they walk away from your voice.

It's not written into your job description. It's not covered in most onboarding packets. But it's there every day, in every interaction. The pressure to deliver. The tension in meetings. The unspoken weight of a team that needs more than direction.

They need presence. They need clarity. They need someone human enough to understand them, not just the mission.

We rarely talk about it because it doesn't sound impressive. But here's the truth that more leaders need to hear: You are not just managing projects. You are managing emotion.

And the moment people feel unsafe, unseen, or unheard, your strategy doesn't matter.

There's a reason why some teams feel heavy, and others feel electric. It's not talent. It's not structure. It's emotional climate.

A culture shaped by fear might deliver compliance. But a culture shaped by care delivers creativity, ownership, and truth.

Because here's the thing:

When people feel safe, they offer their truth. And once they do, the real work of leadership begins.

But when they don't feel safe?

They nod when they disagree.

They say "yes" while quietly checking out.

They do the task, but they leave their brilliance behind.

And what you're left with is a quiet erosion. Not of talent, but of trust.

We like to believe leadership is about certainty. That we're supposed to have the answers. That we need to walk into the room and command respect with the sharpness of our insight or the sharpness of our tone.

But people don't follow your IQ. They follow your presence. They follow the way you navigate stress. The way you handle conflict. The way you respond to fear, not just your own, but theirs.

They follow how you speak when no one else wants to. And how you listen when someone finally gathers the courage to say what needs saying.

I've come to believe that the real test of leadership doesn't happen during performance reviews or after successful project completions. It happens in the quiet moments, the human ones, when life intrudes and suddenly the mission has to share space with mortality, fear, or overwhelming emotion. These are the moments that don't appear on whiteboards or org charts, but they shape your team's trust more than any directive ever could.

One of the earliest lessons I learned came during my deployment to Bosnia. It was 1996, and back then, there was no such thing as instant notification. Word traveled slowly, often through handwritten letters or messages relayed through unofficial channels.

One day, a soldier in our unit learned that his mother had passed a full week earlier. His family had been trying to reach him, but the delay was unavoidable. Grief hit him like a freight train. When he went to his command, still stunned and barely able to process what had happened, the first response he received was clinical, cold, almost inhuman: "Well, she's already passed. It's not as though your presence will bring her back."

I will never forget the stillness that followed those words. And I will never forget the look in that soldier's eyes. He had a full combat load strapped to his body, and no emotional safety net to catch him.

Fortunately, more seasoned and emotionally intelligent voices stepped in. The tone shifted. Compassion finally entered the room. He was pulled from duty, given the space he needed, and expedited home to grieve with his family. But the damage from those first words? That stayed. You could feel it in the silence. A failure of empathy, of timing, of leadership.

Contrast that with an experience years later, when I was stationed in Korea. We were working in a high-output environment, short-staffed like most military units, constantly balancing operational tempo with training schedules. One morning, a soldier on my team, dependable, never complained, never late, showed up behind schedule.

In a place where minutes matter, that alone was notable. But I didn't press. I just asked, "Everything okay?"

He hesitated, looked at the floor, then said quietly, "They think my daughter might need spinal surgery."

No dramatic explanation. No emotion-laced monologue. Just a man carrying something heavy.

I didn't give him a checklist. I didn't ask if his leave paperwork was ready. I told him to go immediately.

We'd figure out the mission. We always did.

What mattered most in that moment was that he knew someone saw him, not just his rank, not just his role. And I'll tell you something—he came back more loyal, more present, and more engaged than ever. Not because I had been generous, but because I had been human.

These moments are where leadership is made or lost.

You don't have to fix everything. You don't have to carry someone else's grief or fear on your back. But if you're not willing to acknowledge it, to stand in it with them even briefly, you'll never earn their full truth. And once a team stops offering you their truth, all you'll ever get is compliance.

There's a version of leadership many of us were taught, especially in uniform.

It was loud.

It was absolute.

And it was rooted in command.

Not connection. Not curiosity. Not care. Just command.

You didn't ask for input. You gave orders.

You didn't explain the "why." You enforced the "what."

You weren't supposed to feel much of anything, and if you did, you damn sure didn't show it.

Because feeling was a liability. Pausing to ask how someone was doing meant slowing down. And slowing down meant something might not get done.

And so, we built entire leadership cultures on the assumption that speed and strength were always the same thing. That toughness meant coldness. That command was synonymous with respect.

But I've lived enough life now, and led enough teams, to know that isn't true.

Command may move people. But connection moves them further.

Command says, "Because I said so."

Connection says, "Here's why this matters, and I believe you're the one to do it."

Command gets compliance.

Connection builds commitment.

Command can get you through a crisis. But connection is what builds a culture people want to be part of, even after the storm has passed.

And here's the hardest part for some to admit: The connection-first leader is just as capable, just as effective, and far more sustainable.

They still get results. They still drive outcomes. But they do it in a way that multiplies their team's energy instead of extracting it. And it shows, in the way their teams talk to one another, in the way they show up when no one is watching, in the way people stay after hours not because they're afraid, but because they're invested.

The command model will always have its place. In moments of crisis, it has utility. But if command is the only tool in your kit, you'll wear out your team and yourself.

The real leaders?

They learn when to give direction, and when to give space.

They learn when to set expectations, and when to check in.

They learn that their strength isn't in being the loudest voice in the room. It's in being the clearest one.

And the clearest voices? They don't just speak to the task.

They speak to the person.

Reflection: What People Remember

In the end, people rarely remember what you said in a meeting.

They remember how they felt walking out of it.

They remember if you made room for their doubt.

They remember whether they could ask the question without fear.

They remember if they were treated like a person, or like a part.

That's why the best leadership doesn't leave a list of completed tasks.

It leaves a trail of people who became more confident, more capable, and more human because of how you treated them.

Because when people feel safe, they tell you the truth.

And when people trust you with their truth, that's when the real work begins.

So before you ask someone to perform, ask yourself:

Have I earned the kind of trust that lets them bring their full self to this task?

Before you correct someone, ask yourself:

Do they believe I see their effort, or just their errors?

Before you lead, ask:

Am I showing up as a person worth following?

The title might say leader.

But the day will reveal the truth.

And if your presence creates space for others to speak, grow, and own their voice, then you're not just running a team.

You're building one.

Conclusion

To Lead, First Be Human

Leadership begins in unexpected places.

For me, it began at a race I officiated poorly. Not because I didn't know better, but because I was still learning what it meant to carry a title with integrity.

It continued in a quiet act of service, when a Sergeant Major made the coffee I didn't want to make, and in doing so, taught me that humility doesn't diminish leadership. It defines it.

It deepened each time I failed forward, grew into my responsibilities, and chose to earn the weight of a role instead of hiding behind its rank.

And it came full circle not in a conference room or a promotion ceremony, but in the human moments:

The grief of a soldier far from home.

The silence after an unfair dismissal.

The quiet thank-you of a teammate who just needed to feel seen.

Those are the real milestones.

Because leadership isn't forged in strategy.

It's built in the space between decisions.

In the way we treat people when no one's taking notes.

We chase frameworks and playbooks, but the truth is much simpler and much harder. You lead by how you show up.

In the hard moments.

The quiet ones.

The ones that ask you to listen longer, to respond softer, to care deeper.

What I've learned, across three decades, multiple countries, and enough failure to know what growth actually costs, is this:

You don't need to be perfect.

You don't need to have all the answers.

You just need to be human.

Because when you are, when you lead from that place of grounded, clear, intentional care, people follow.

Not because they have to.

But because they want to.

Because they trust that your presence makes them better, stronger, safer.

And that trust is the only kind of power that multiplies when you give it away.

So, take the coffee.

Take the criticism.

Take the small chance to lift someone when no one's watching.

Do it not because it's your job.

Do it because it's your calling.

Because in the end, titles fade.

Awards collect dust.

And nobody remembers your PowerPoint slides.

They remember how they felt when you walked into the room.

They remember if your leadership made space for their voice.

They remember whether you chose command or connection.

And if you've done it right, if you've truly led with presence, with intention, with humanity, they won't just remember you. They'll become leaders worth remembering too.

So let this be your charge:

Don't lead for recognition. Lead for resonance.

Don't lead to impress. Lead to empower.

Don't lead like a savior. Lead like a steward.

Because at the end of every strategy, behind every mission, inside every system, are people.

And people don't give their best to authority. They give it to trust.

So, if you remember nothing else, remember this:

To lead, first be human—because only when people feel seen, heard, and valued will they give you their best, and trust you with their truth.

Coming Soon: Keep Walking
How Small Steps Build a Big Life

From the author of *To Lead, First Be Human* comes a deeply personal follow-up, designed to help you move forward through resistance, rebuild rhythm, and walk your way through uncertainty with presence and purpose.

Leadership doesn't end with understanding people.

It continues with understanding yourself, especially in the quiet moments after the applause fades.

In *Keep Walking*, Dr. Tru Notoma turns inward to explore the questions that follow every courageous act of human-centered leadership:

How do you keep going when life interrupts your rhythm?

How do you rebuild trust in yourself after setbacks?

How do you make progress when motivation is gone but the mission remains?

This follow-up to *To Lead, First Be Human* offers more than inspiration. It delivers rhythm.

Drawing from a lifetime of service across continents, from fast-food kitchens and military bases to boardrooms and doctoral programs, Tru introduces the W.A.L.K. framework:

- W – Why You Started
- A – Accountability to Progress
- L – Legacy Through Consistency
- K – Keep Walking

Through vivid stories, actionable insights, and the same grounded humanity that made his first book a trusted companion, Tru offers a clear reminder: you don't need to sprint. You just need to walk. And walk again.

From Chapter One of *Keep Walking*:

"Every job gave me a schedule, a uniform, a paycheck, but none of it gave me a vision.

There were slivers of clarity that told me I was wasting potential, not just time.

I wasn't failing at work. I was failing at motion.

And the only way forward was to stop performing and start becoming again, one small step at a time."

If *To Lead, First Be Human* helped you lead others with care,

Keep Walking will help you lead yourself with rhythm, courage, and the resilience to rise.

Stay in rhythm. Be the first to read it.

Visit my author profile on Amazon to join early readers and get launch updates.

Dr. Ogheneotsuko "Tru" Notoma

www.ingramcontent.com/pod-product-compliance
Lightning Source LLC
Chambersburg PA
CBHW050249010526
44107CB00003B/250